MORE PRAISE FOR SECRET IDENTITIES...

Good fiction opens a window into truth. And really good fiction opens a window into truths you never thought of before. This book is a new window on a rarely seen side of the American experience. Take a look through it. You'll be surprised.

—Walter Simonson, writer/artist, MANHUNTER, THOR and ORION

SECRET IDENTITIES has hit upon one of those truths that feels surprising only because no one thought of it sooner: that our culture's superhero template dovetails uncannily with Asian American issues and identity.

—David Henry Hwang, playwright, M. BUTTERFLY and GOLDEN CHILD

This book will acquaint new audiences to the Asian American experience and inspire younger generations to explore their own history, identity and culture.

—Irene Hirano Inouye, executive adviser, Japanese American National Museum

These artists show how to be funny and witty and profound all at once, turning stereotypes inside out and upside down to create new images that empower individuals to write the scripts of their own lives. A classic on the level of MAUS and THE DARK KNIGHT RETURNS, this is a comic book every Asian American teenager needs to read, every Asian American adult should buy, and every person of any background will appreciate.

—Frank H. Wu, author, YELLOW: RACE IN AMERICA BEYOND BLACK AND WHITE

Where were these comics when I was a kid? At long last, here are the Asian American superheroes I've always wanted. Make no mistake, these are geeky comic book stories. But they're our geeky comic book stories. And that makes all the difference.

—Phil Yu, AngryAsianMan.com

Compilation © 2009 by Jeff Yang, Parry Shen, Keith Chow, and Jerry Ma
Individual pieces © 2009 by each creator

Requests for permission to reproduce selections from this book should be mailed to:

Permissions Department, The New Press, 38 Greene Street, New York, NY 10013.

Published in the United States by The New Press, New York, 2009
Distributed by Perseus Distribution

CIP data available.
978-1-59558-398-7 (Pbk.)

The New Press was established in 1990 as a not-for-profit alternative to the large, commercial publishing houses currently dominating the book publishing industry. The New Press operates in the public interest rather than for private gain, and is committed to publishing, in innovative ways, works of educational, cultural, and community value that are often deemed insufficiently profitable.

www.thenewpress.com

Book design and composition by Jerry Ma

Printed in Canada

10 9 8 7 6 5 4 3 2 1

SECRET iDENTITIES

The Asian American Superhero Anthology

JEFF YANG
PARRY SHEN
KEITH CHOW
JERRY MA

THE NEW PRESS

NEW YORK
LONDON

CONTENTS

CONTENTS

EDITOR IN CHIEF: JEFF YANG
MANAGING EDITOR: PARRY SHEN
EDITOR AT LARGE: KEITH CHOW
ART DIRECTOR: JERRY MA
SENIOR ARTIST: JEF CASTRO

WWW.SECRETIDENTITIES.ORG

ACKNOWLEDGMENTS

The editors would like to thank the many talented creators whose contributions made this book possible, as well as those whose imagination and dedication to the craft first inspired it.

Special gratitude should be extended to our editors at the New Press, Andy Hsiao and Sarah Fan (of whom we're number-one fans)—as well as to our families, who bore this two-year journey with patience, grace, and love.

Also: John Fisk for giving us glasses, Larry Hama for paving the way, DC, Marvel, and United Media for graciously allowing us to use some of their characters and creators, and our fifth Beatle, senior artist Jef Castro, for his indomitable good nature, nose-to-the-grindstone attitude, and brilliant artwork.

And finally, to our kids—because, ultimately, this is for them.

SECRET IDENTITIES BABIES

Keina Kojima Chow, July 3, 2007
Skyler Jordan Yang, February 24, 2008
Kori Layne Shen, March 18, 2008
Klee Hyoun Kang, September 19, 2008
Emi Hope Quiogue Sperber, January 12, 2009

story by: Jeff Yang — art by: Jef Castro

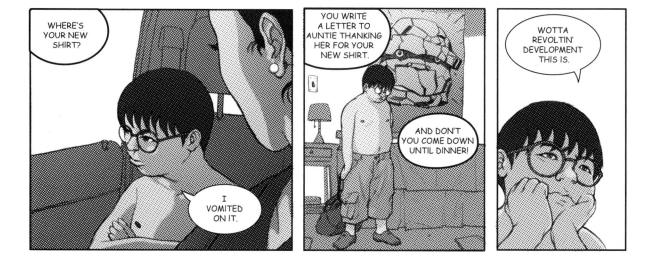

WHERE'S YOUR NEW SHIRT?

I VOMITED ON IT.

YOU WRITE A LETTER TO AUNTIE THANKING HER FOR YOUR NEW SHIRT.

AND DON'T YOU COME DOWN UNTIL DINNER!

WOTTA REVOLTIN' DEVELOPMENT THIS IS.

25 YEARS LATER...

ARE YOU COMING TO BED, HON?

IN A MINUTE--

--I'M DOING AN INTERVIEW...

HELLO?

HEY, KEITH? THIS IS JEFF--

--I'M WRITING A COLUMN ABOUT ASIAN SUPERHEROES,

SURE-- --SHOOT.

SO... WHAT'S THE DEAL WITH HOLLYWOOD'S CURRENT FASCINATION WITH SUPERHEROES?

AND I EMAILED YOU ABOUT AN INTERVIEW...

WELL, I THINK IT'S BECAUSE SUPERHEROES ARE SO INGRAINED INTO POPULAR CULTURE

THAT WHEN A SUPERMAN OR X-MEN MOVIE COMES OUT, EVEN PEOPLE WHO'VE NEVER READ A COMIC BOOK IN THEIR LIVES ARE ALREADY FAMILIAR WITH THEM.

THEY'RE NOT JUST CARTOON CHARACTERS--

--THEY'RE MODERN AMERICAN MYTHOLOGY.

SO THEY'RE THE NEW GREEK MYTHS?

YEAH, ONLY MORE PERSONAL.

GREEK KIDS COULDN'T DREAM OF GROWING UP TO BE HERCULES,

BUT LOOK AT SPIDER-MAN!

--HE'S THIS ORDINARY, GEEKY KID WHO GETS BITTEN BY A RADIOACTIVE SPIDER.

AND SO, IT BEGINS...

story by: Jeff Yang - art by: Benton Jew

16

GO!
GODDAMMIT, THAT AIN'T POSSIBLE.
I DON'T KNOW WHAT PLOT YOU AND THAT DAMN DANDY PARDEE COOKED UP, BUT IT COST ME MORE'N YOU TWO ARE WORTH.

17

SEEMS TO ME YOU SHOULD BLAME TH' CHINAMAN. STOLE IN THERE FOR THE LIQUOR, I'D SAY. YOU CAN SMELL IT ON 'IM.

I'LL TELL YOU WHAT, CREEDER: ONE MORE CONTEST. IF YOUR MEN WIN, I WON'T MENTION THE STOREHOUSE IN MY REPORT, AND I'LL GIVE YOU BACK YOUR MONEY.

AND IF YOU WIN? I AIN'T GOT NO MORE TO LOSE.

THE BOY AND THE CHINAMAN. I WIN, I'M BRINGING THEM BACK EAST.

DONE. SICK OF 'EM BOTH ANYWAY. BUT / CLAIM RIGHT TO CHOOSE TH' GAME....

WE'RE AT TH' FOOT OF IRON MOUNTAIN RIGHT NOW. TOO WIDE T'GO AROUND, TOO STEEP T'GO OVER, SO WE BEEN CUTTIN' THROUGH. TWO TEAMS'LL FINISH THE JOB, A SETTER AND A DRIVER FOR EACH TUNNEL. WHOEVER COMES OUT 'TOTHER SIDE FIRST WINS.

THAT'S HARDLY A FAIR CONTEST. THE CELESTIALS? THEY'VE GOT PLUCK, BUT THEY HAVEN'T THE BRAWN OF YOUR IRISH.

SIZE IN'T EVERYTHING.

WE'LL BEAT CREEDER FOR YOU, SUH, ME AND JIMSON.

BANG!

WATER, SUH?

NO...NEVER WATER.

WHY AIN'T YOU LIKE THE OTHER CHINEE? WHAT MAKES YOU... *DIFFERENT?*

MY...PEOPLE...ARE FROM THE FAR WEST OF CHINA, A PLACE CALLED THE BURNING MOUNTAIN— *FO JIM SAAN.*

story and art by: Tak Toyoshima

story by: Jonathan Tsuei - art by: Jerry Ma

27

"BEFORE I SIGNED UP, MY DAD ASKED ME *WHY* I WANTED TO FIGHT."

SATURDAY POST CITIZEN NEWSREEL

MOVIE TONE NEWS: AMERICA AT WAR

"...I DIDN'T HAVE AN *ANSWER* FOR HIM AT THE TIME."

SATURDAY POST CITIZEN NEWSREEL

JAPANESE AMERICAN INTERNEES FILING INTO CAMP

THE 100TH BATTALION, AMERICA'S ALL-JAPANESE SQUADRON, AS THEY MARCH OFF TO GERMANY TO FIGHT THE GOOD FIGHT!

WORLD WAR II. *GERMANY, 1944.*

"MY NAME IS *JAMES IMAMURA.* UNITED STATES ARMY. PRIVATE FIRST CLASS... *SECOND CLASS CITIZEN.*"

"JUST ANOTHER ORDINARY *NISEI GRUNT....*"

"OKAY, WELL, MAYBE NOT SO *ORDINARY.*"

"THEY CALL US THE *SUNSET SQUAD.*"

"WE'RE THE *METAHUMAN* TASK FORCE OF THE *100TH BATTALION.* YOU WON'T SEE US IN ANY *NEWSREELS*...WE DO THE KIND OF MISSIONS YOU'D ONLY HEAR ABOUT IF WE *FAILED.*"

story by: Daniel Jai Lee - art by: Vince Sunico

"A YEAR LATER, WHEN THE ARMY ANNOUNCED THEY WERE FORMING *SUNSET SQUAD*, HE CALLED IN A *FAVOR* AND GOT HIS *TRAIN TRACKS* BACK. SERVING THE COUNTRY HE *LOVES* IS THE ONLY THING HE EVER KNEW HOW TO DO..."

IMAMURA, THROW A COVER ON *WATADA*. LET HIM RUN HIS *HEAD* AGAINST THAT *WALL* AND SEE WHICH BREAKS FIRST.

THANKS, CAP... YOU'RE *ALL HEART*.

"GUESS HE FELT WE WERE THE ONLY WAY HE COULD STILL DO IT WITH *HONOR*."

"*YUJI WATADA'S* REASONS FOR JOINING WERE VERY DIFFERENT. HE WAS VISITING RELATIVES IN *TOKYO* WHEN *PEARL HARBOR* WAS HIT."

"THEY PUT HIM THROUGH A *NASTY* SET OF *EXPERIMENTS* THAT GAVE HIM *SUPER STRENGTH* AND NEARLY *UNBREAKABLE SKIN*."

"WHEN THEY COULDN'T GET HIM TO *FLIP*, THEY DRUGGED HIM AND PUT HIM IN A *KAMIKAZE ZERO*. HE SURVIVED A 10,000-FOOT FALL ONTO AN AMERICAN CARRIER DECK WITHOUT A *PARACHUTE*, AND WAS ARRESTED AS A *JAPANESE SPY*."

"WATADA SPENT *SIX MONTHS* IN JAIL, UNTIL THE ARMY GAVE HIM A WAY TO *PROVE* HIS LOYALTY: *US*."

GUYS...WE GOT A *PROBLEM*.

"HANK YOSHI IS OUR MEDIC. IF YOU AIN'T DEAD, HIS POWERS CAN HEAL YOU."

"HE SAID HE SIGNED UP TO SAVE AS MANY NISEI LIVES AS HE COULD. LORD KNOWS HOW MANY TIMES HE'S SAVED ME."

THWAAK

"THE UBERS. JOE MENGELE'S MONSTER KIDS."

NICE OF YOU TO STOP BY—WE'VE BEEN EXPECTING YOU.

SORRY YOUR VISIT WILL BE SO SHORT.

POWW

"THEY WERE WAITING FOR US. IT WAS A TRAP."

KRAK

THOK

"UBERMENSCH."

"ONE OF THE MOST POWERFUL METAHUMANS IN THE WORLD. POSTER BOY FOR THE ARYAN RACE."

story by: Jamie Ford - art by: Alexander Tarampi

37

39

story by: Keith Chow – art by: A.L. Baroza

story by: Greg Pak – art by: Bernard Chang

RASSIN FRASSIN...

FOR WHAT IT'S WORTH, YOU WOULDN'T TECHNICALLY BE WORKING FOR THE *GOVERNMENT*. YOU'D BE MORE OF A... FREELANCER, REPORTING DIRECTLY TO--

I'M NOT A BODYGUARD.

I WISH IT WERE THAT SIMPLE.

THE FIRST THING I DID WHEN I TOOK OFFICE WAS ASK FOR THE... *INTERESTING* FILES.

COME ON. LIKE THEY'RE GONNA SHOW AREA 51 TO *YOU*.

EXACTLY.

BUT MY PREDECESSOR LEFT A FEW PASSWORDS ON A STICK-IT NOTE IN THE PRESIDENTIAL PENCIL DRAWER.

AND THE VERY *LITTLE* I'VE BEEN ABLE TO DISCOVER AS A RESULT MAKES ME REALIZE HOW *CRITICAL* IT IS TO FIND OUT THE *REST*.

FOR EXAMPLE...

MICKEY LELAND. RON BROWN. OTIS REDDING. AALIYAH.

AFRICAN AMERICAN POLITICIANS AND POP STARS KILLED IN SMALL AIRPLANE CRASHES. THAT'S WHAT YOU'RE WORRIED ABOUT?

YOU FLY IN *BIG* PLANES, DON'T YOU?

DAMN STRAIGHT.

BUT IT DOESN'T MUCH MATTER...

... WHEN YOU'RE UP AGAINST *GREMLINS*.

GREMLINS?

ACTUALLY...

story by: Keith Chow – art by: A.L. Baroza

SIDEKICKS: GENE YANG & MICHAEL KANG

"HONESTLY, I WAS NEVER A *FAN* OF THE *GREEN HORNET*."

YES, BOSS.

YOU HAVE THIS HANDSOME, WEALTHY CRIMEFIGHTER, AND THE ASIAN MARTIAL ARTS EXPERT IS HIS *CHAUFFEUR*? I MEAN, IT'S *DEMEANING*.

GENE YANG, CREATOR OF *AMERICAN BORN CHINESE*

YA KNOW, *BRUCE LEE* ACTUALLY FELT THE SAME WAY.

MICHAEL KANG, ACCLAIMED DIRECTOR OF *THE MOTEL* AND *WEST 32ND*.

THAT MIGHT BE THE CASE, BUT THE UNFORTUNATE LEGACY OF *KATO* IS THAT HE WAS JUST THE "*SIDEKICK*" AT A TIME WHEN SIDEKICKS WERE *KIDS IN SHORTS* WHO FOLLOWED THE HERO AROUND.

TALK ABOUT *EMASCULATING*.

IT'S A NON-THREATENING WAY FOR THE *MAINSTREAM* TO ACCEPT THE "*ALIEN*"—

ASIANS ARE *FINE* AS LONG AS THERE'S A *WHITE GUY* AROUND TO TAKE THE *LEAD*.

IRONIC, SINCE BRUCE LEE WAS THE EPITOME OF *MASCULINITY*—

CHARISMATIC, GOOD LOOKING, *ARTICULATE*...

BUT MARKETING EXECS HAVE NO IDEA HOW TO SELL AN *ASIAN* AS THE *HERO*, SO THEY DON'T THINK IT CAN BE *DONE*.

THAT'S WHY, TO THIS DAY, WE HAVE TO FIGHT OFF THE *DESCENDANTS* OF KATO.

EVEN *DOCTOR STRANGE* HAD A *CHINESE SERVANT*. MAN, ARE *ALL* ASIANS EXOTIC MARTIAL ARTS EXPERTS?

DON'T FORGET— SOME MARTIAL ARTISTS ARE *WHITE GUYS* WHO JUST HAPPEN TO HAVE *MYSTICAL FIGHTING ABILITIES*.

SO? SOME OF MY *BEST FRIENDS* ARE ASIAN.

LIKE IT OR NOT, THE LEGACY OF KATO IS *INGRAINED* IN OUR POP CULTURE *ZEITGEIST*.

THAT'S WHY IT'S IMPORTANT TO DO WHAT *BRUCE* DID. TELL OUR *OWN* STORIES, ON OUR *OWN* TERMS.

THE MORE OF US THERE ARE *OUT THERE* TELLING OUR STORIES, THE MORE *MULTIFACETED, COMPLEX* ASIAN CHARACTERS WE'LL SEE.

ONE THING'S FOR SURE, IF BRUCE HAD NEVER GOTTEN *FED UP* WITH ROLES LIKE KATO, HE MIGHT NOT HAVE GONE BACK TO *HONG KONG*,

AND THE WORLD WOULD HAVE BEEN WITHOUT THE *TRUE* LEGACY OF *BRUCE LEE*.

GOOD POINT.

story by: Gene Yang — art by: Sonny Liew

story by: Michael Kang – art by: Erwin Haya

YOU PROBABLY REMEMBER ME FROM THE *OLD DAYS*. THAT IS, IF YOU REMEMBER ME AT *ALL*.

IN THE BEGINNING, IT WASN'T THE "*HUMAN LIGHT*," CAPITAL *H*, CAPITAL *L*, THOUGH. AND I WASN'T *TWINKLE* BACK THEN. HE WAS JUST *HANK*, AND I WAS *JAMES*. BUT THE PRESS HAS A WAY OF SPINNING STUFF TO MAKE IT MORE...*MARKETABLE*.

I FIRST MET HANK BACK IN *COLLEGE*. I FELT BAD FOR THE GUY. HE WANTED TO BE A SUPERHERO, BUT ALL HE COULD DO WAS *EMIT LIGHT*. I'M NOT TALKING ABOUT LASERS, EITHER; HE COULD BASICALLY...*GLOW*. HIS POWER TOPPED OUT AT ABOUT *400 LUMENS*—60-WATT LIGHTBULB TERRITORY. IT LOOKED PRETTY COOL, BUT LET'S FACE IT...IT WASN'T ALL THAT *SUPER*.

SEE?

PRETTY COOL. UH... IS THAT IT?

WOW!

WOW!

MAN, WE SHOULD *TOTALLY* TEAM UP!

I HAD *SUPER-AGILITY*, *SUPER-STRENGTH*, AND A DEGREE IN *FORENSICS*, SO I DID MOST OF THE HEAVY LIFTING. IT JUST MADE SENSE. AND IT WAS ALL *GOOD*...FOR A *WHILE*.

BUT YOU KNOW, *SUCCESS* CHANGES EVERYTHING.

HUMAN LIGHT AND TWINKLE

HUMAN LIGHT AND TWINKLE THE MOVIE

HEROES FOR THE HUNGRY

PEOPLE GOT NO FOOD AND IT JUST AIN'T RIGHT...

CAUSE STARVATION IS AS DEADLY AS KRYPTONITE...

SO LET'S SHED SOME LIGHT... ON A BIGGER FIGHT...WE'RE HEROES...FOR THE HUNGRY...

AS SOON AS THE PUBLIC STARTED TO *NOTICE* WHAT WE WERE DOING, WE HAD TO HIRE AN AGENT, A PUBLICIST, A STYLIST...THERE WAS NO WAY WE COULD KEEP UP WITH THE THINGS COMING IN ON OUR *OWN*. I'M TALKING DEALS FOR COMIC BOOKS, MOVIES, TOYS...WE EVEN CUT A *CD* FOR *CHARITY*.

STARTING OVER WASN'T EASY. I WENT TO *N.O.A.S.S.** NETWORKING EVENTS, BUT THEY WERE FILLED WITH *OTHER* GUYS WHO COULDN'T FIND ANY CRIME TO FIGHT. THEY WERE BASICALLY *MEAT MARKETS* FOR MIDDLE-AGED HEROES WITH MARRIED SECRET IDENTITIES. THE WHOLE SCENE WAS PRETTY *DEPRESSING.*

* NATIONAL ORGANIZATION OF ASIAN SUPERS AND SIDEKICKS

I KNEW I HAD A STRONG BASE WITH THE *COLLEGE KIDS.* BUT THE *HONORARIUMS* FOR SAVING KIDS ON CAMPUS REALLY WEREN'T PAYING THE RENT. THE BIGGEST SAVE I DID WAS AT *A.S.S.H.O** 2006, WHEN I TOOK ON THE *DISORIENTER.*

PAGE 17—OTHER NEWS: STUDENT GATHERING SHUT DOWN BY LOCAL POLICE DUE TO NOISE COMPLAINTS

IT WAS A BIG HIT WITH THE KIDS, BUT LET'S JUST SAY THAT AN ASIAN *HERO* SAVING ASIAN *VICTIMS* FROM AN ASIAN *VILLAIN* DOESN'T EXACTLY MAKE THE FRONT PAGE HEADLINES.

* ASIAN STUDENT SUPER HERO ORGANIZATION

I TRIED FOCUSING ON SAVING ONLY *NON-ASIANS* FOR A WHILE, BUT THAT FELT *WRONG.*

MY HERO!

IT WAS ALSO TOUGH TO GET SOME OF THE MORE HIGH-PROFILE *VICTIMS* TO TAKE ME *SERIOUSLY.*

OH NO, *THIS* WON'T DO.

story by: Keith Chow – art by: Alexander Shen

BALTIMORE, 1963.

TODAY.

I GREW UP IN ONE OF THE *POOREST NEIGHBORHOODS* YOU COULD IMAGINE. THE ONE THING I AND MY BEST FRIENDS *TIMMY* AND *RICHARD* HAD IN COMMON WAS *COMIC BOOKS.*

BUT AS MUCH AS I *LOVED* THEM, I DON'T THINK I REALLY *RELATED* TO ANY OF MY FAVORITE COMIC BOOK CHARACTERS. AND I CAN'T RECALL *EVER* SEEING A SINGLE *FILIPINO* CHARACTER IN A MAINSTREAM AMERICAN COMIC.

COMICS MADE GETTING THROUGH THE *TOUGH TIMES* EASIER. THEY WERE ALL ABOUT *OVERCOMING CHALLENGES,* ABOUT *GOOD* TRIUMPHING OVER *EVIL.* ABOUT DOING YOUR BEST TO *CHANGE THE WORLD.*

GREG LAROCQUE, COMIC ARTIST, "THE FLASH"

I DON'T THINK IT'S BECAUSE OF *CONSCIOUS* BIAS. IN COMICS, THE *STUFF* YOU DO STANDS ON ITS *OWN.* PEOPLE JUDGE YOU PURELY ON YOUR *ABILITY* AND THE *WORK* YOU'RE PRODUCING.

YOU CAN EVEN GO BACK TO THE *EARLY '80s,* WHEN A SLEW OF *FILIPINO INKERS* LIKE *RUDY NEBRES* AND *TONY DEZUNIGA* WORKED AT *MARVEL.* IT'S ALWAYS BEEN AN INDUSTRY WHERE REALLY TALENTED PEOPLE OF *ANY BACKGROUND* HAVE HAD THE OPPORTUNITY TO *EXCEL.*

THE REASON WHY SO MANY *ASIAN AMERICAN* ARTISTS, PEOPLE LIKE *JIM LEE* AND *JAE LEE,* ARE AT THE TOP OF OUR PROFESSION, IS BECAUSE THEY'RE *GOOD.*

BUT THAT HASN'T NECESSARILY SHOWN UP ON THE *PRINTED PAGE*—SO, OVER THE LAST 10 OR 20 YEARS, THERE'S BEEN THIS REAL EFFORT TO SAY, "WE'VE GOT TO TREAT OUR STORIES WITH A LITTLE MORE *MATURITY.*" TO MAKE THEM LOOK MORE LIKE THE *REAL WORLD.*

I WAS RIGHT IN THE *MIDDLE* OF THIS *DIVERSITY PUSH* IN THE '80S AND '90S, THOUGH I WISH I COULD CLAIM *CREDIT* FOR IT.

NOW.

BUT I'VE STILL NEVER SEEN AN ORIGINAL *FILIPINO* CHARACTER IN A COMIC HERE IN THE *STATES.* THAT'S WHY THIS PROJECT INTERESTED ME SO MUCH, AND WHY IT WAS SO GREAT TO DO A STORY THAT DEALS WITH THINGS I CARE *ABOUT.* IT MAY NOT CHANGE THE WORLD...

MY ONLY RESPONSIBILITY WAS MAKING SURE THAT CHARACTERS LIKE *LINDA PARK,* WALLY *"THE FLASH"* WEST'S GIRLFRIEND, WERE DEPICTED REALISTICALLY. I ALWAYS SAW LINDA AS THE *ASIAN AMERICAN LOIS LANE*—A *REAL PERSON,* NOT A *STEREOTYPE.*

BUT THERE WAS *NOTHING* OUT THERE, AND NOW THERE *IS.* AND THAT'S *REALLY COOL.*

THE FRUITS OF WAR ARE NOT JUST *DEATH*. SOMETIMES *LIFE*, TOO, SPRINGS FROM THE FURROWS OF DESTRUCTION. AND THAT LIFE IS A LEGACY WHICH, IF *UNACKNOWLEDGED*, CAN BREED CONFUSION, PREJUDICE...EVEN A THIRST FOR *VENGEANCE*.

TRINITY

story and art by: Greg LaRocque

"WE SHAPE OUR *LIVES* NOT BY WHAT WE *CARRY* WITH US, BUT BY WHAT WE *LEAVE BEHIND*."

—ANONYMOUS

THREE TIMES A **WARRIOR**: SKIN OF **STEEL**. SHADOW WALKER. **EYES** TO SEE **BEYOND**.

THREE TIMES A **LOVER**: SOWER OF **SEEDS**, GROWN WHOLE AND **TRUE**. BUT ALONE. **UNKNOWN**.

GONE, BUT LIVING ON— HIS MEASURE **DIVIDED** AND **DIVIDED** AND **DIVIDED**.

THREE TIMES.

"I HAVE HAD **VISIONS** SINCE I WAS A CHILD...OF A MAN, A **HERO**, WHO CIRCLED THE WORLD TO BATTLE **EVIL**. THREE TIMES HE NEARLY LOST HIS **LIFE**; THREE TIMES, HE LEFT A LIFE **BEHIND**."

"WHAT THIS MEANS I CAN ONLY **SUSPECT**—BUT HIS **RELATIONSHIP** TO ME IS CLEAR. HE WAS MY **FATHER**. AND FROM HIM, I INHERITED...**POWER**."

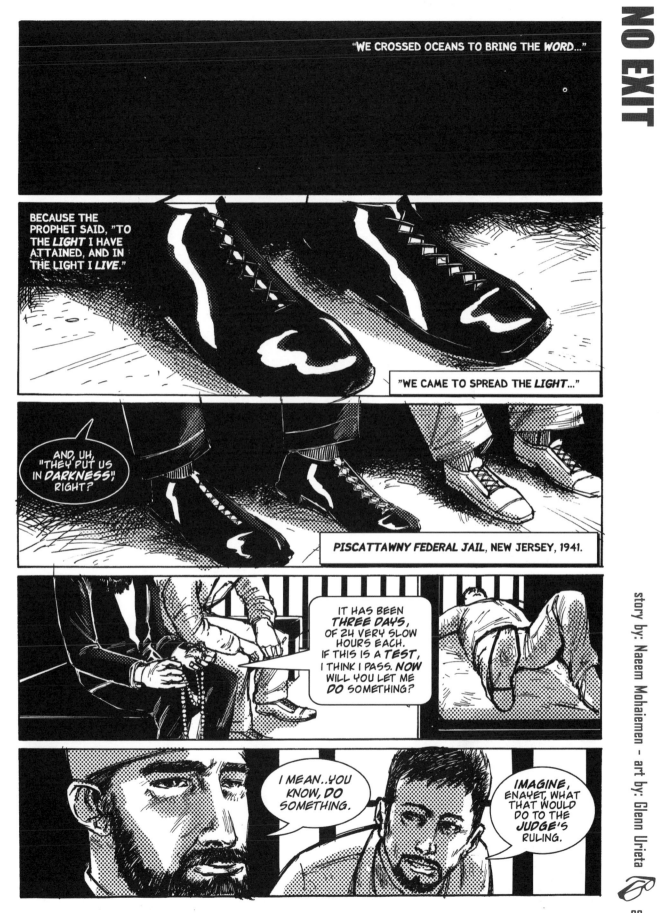

"WE CROSSED OCEANS TO BRING THE *WORD*..."

BECAUSE THE PROPHET SAID, "TO THE *LIGHT* I HAVE ATTAINED, AND IN THE LIGHT I *LIVE*."

"WE CAME TO SPREAD THE *LIGHT*..."

AND, UH, "THEY PUT US IN *DARKNESS*" RIGHT?

PISCATTAWNY FEDERAL JAIL, NEW JERSEY, 1941.

IT HAS BEEN *THREE DAYS*, OF 24 VERY SLOW HOURS EACH. IF THIS IS A *TEST*, I THINK I PASS. *NOW* WILL YOU LET ME *DO* SOMETHING?

I MEAN..YOU KNOW, *DO* SOMETHING.

IMAGINE, ENAYET, WHAT THAT WOULD DO TO THE *JUDGE'S* RULING.

story by: Naeem Mohaiemen – art by: Glenn Urieta

91

story by: Tanuj Chopra - art by: Alex Joon Kim

story by: Lynn Chen – art by: Paul Wei

101

story by: Jimmy Aquino – art by: Erwin Haya

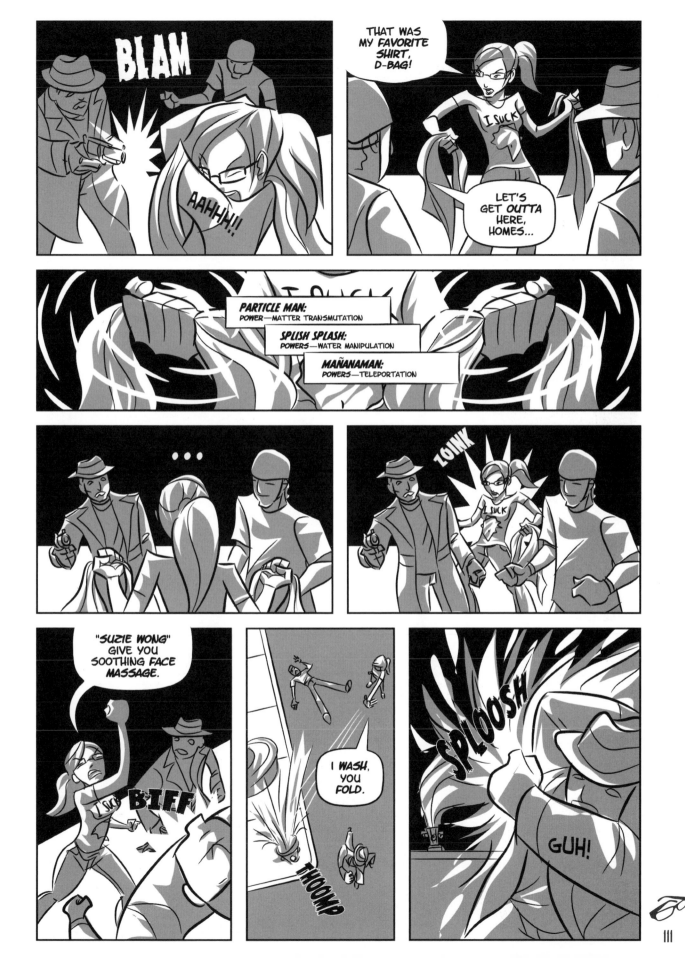

115

story by: Jeff Yang - art by: A.L. Baroza

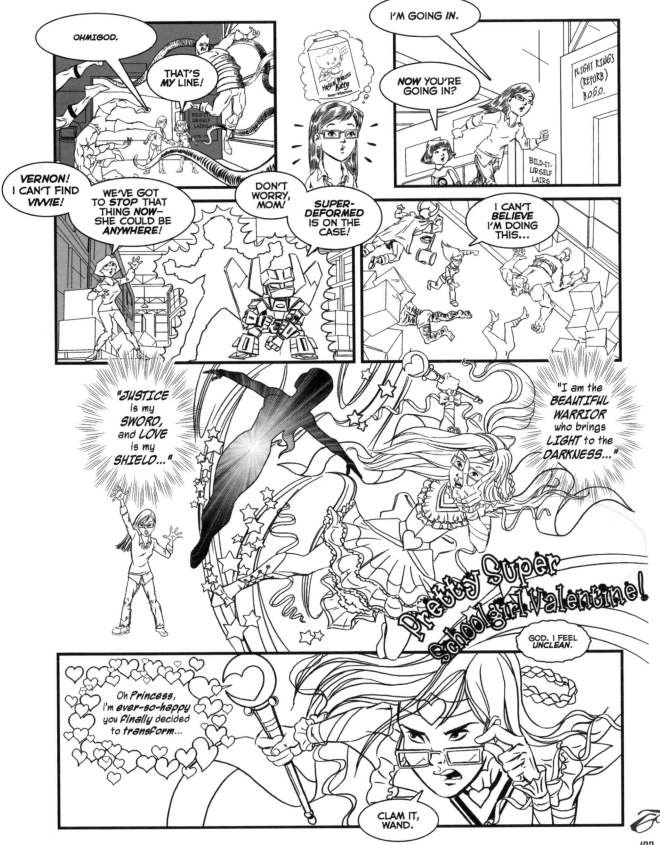

SUPERGRRRLS

story and art by: Hellen Jo

YOU KNOW WHAT **ANNOYS** ME? COMICS WHERE **GIRLS** ARE PORTRAYED AS WEAK, HELPLESS, AND IN NEED OF A **HERO**. THAT'S JUST **RIDICULOUS**. AND **INSULTING**.

SO I AVOID 'EM. THE COMICS **I** READ HAVE FEMALE CHARACTERS THAT ARE STRONG-WILLED, INDEPENDENT, AND INTELLIGENT. LIKE **"GHOST WORLD,"** OR EVEN **"PEANUTS"**! THESE ARE GIRLS WHO CAN TAKE CARE OF **THEMSELVES**, AND WHO DON'T SUFFER FOOLS GLADLY.

IN JAIME HERNANDEZ'S **"LOVE & ROCKETS,"** THERE'S A CHARACTER NAMED **DAFFY**, A TIMID ASIAN AMERICAN TEEN WHO STUMBLES INTO THE **PUNK SCENE**, BLEACHES HER HAIR, AND MAKES NEW MOHAWKED FRIENDS.

EVENTUALLY, THOUGH, SHE SHEDS HER PUNK WAYS, GOES OFF TO UCLA, AND BECOMES AN **OPTOMETRIST**.

THAT'S AN **EERILY ACCURATE** REPRESENTATION OF MANY SUBURBAN ASIAN AMERICAN GIRLS I GREW UP WITH--EVEN **MYSELF**, TO SOME DEGREE.

IN HIGH SCHOOL, WE TRIED TO LOOK LIKE **PUNKS** AND **GOTHS**, TO SEEM **TOUGHER** TO OUR FAMILIES, OUR FRIENDS, AND OURSELVES. BUT HAVING LIVED **SHELTERED LIVES**, WE REALIZE IT'S JUST A **COSTUME**, AND GROW OUT OF IT.

THAT'S PART OF WHY **SUPERHEROES** ARE APPEALING... THEY **NEVER** GROW OUT OF THEIR COSTUMES.

MY **FAVORITE** HERO IS **FANTOMAH**, MYSTERY WOMAN OF THE JUNGLE, FROM **FLETCHER HANKS'** BIZARRE COMICS OF THE '40S. FANTOMAH PROTECTS THE "JUNGLE-BORN" FROM **SCHEMING MEN** WHO WANT TO EXPLOIT THE JUNGLE FOR ITS JEWELS, PANTHERS, AND **GIGANTIC SPIDERS**.

HERE'S MY HERO:

THE BRAZEN RAISIN.

SHE DEFENDS **HARRIED STUDENTS** FROM THE OVERBEARING EXPECTATIONS OF **WELL-MEANING PARENTS**--

--HOLDING OFF MOM AND DAD WHILE **JOHNNY** AND **JANIE** EXPLORE INTERESTS OUTSIDE THE REALM OF **S.A.T. TESTING**, WHETHER THEY BE **BRAIN SURGERY** OR **COMIC BOOK** ILLUSTRATION.

SHE RESEMBLES **MARLENE DIETRICH**, BUT WHEN ENRAGED, HER FACE CHANGES INTO A HORRIFYING GREY SKULL. ODDLY, SHE STILL RETAINS HER **BLONDE CURLS** AND **BANGIN' BODY**.

HOW COULD YOU **NOT** LOVE A WOMAN WITH A **SKULL FOR A FACE** WHO FLIES AROUND PROTECTING **INDIGENOUS PEOPLE**?

HJ '08

CHARACTER
GALLERY

agent orange

A Vietnamese American mercenary trapped in an explosion of cached armaments and defoliants from the war, gives birth to a gruesome "offspring"—a misshapen creature that murders the man's lover and begins systematically hunting down his employers. But as the soldier ruthlessly pursues his nemesis, it becomes less clear which of the two is the true monster—and whether the creature's objective is murder or penance for a lifetime of bloodshed and betrayal.

CONCEPT BY:
DUSTIN TRI NGUYEN

ART BY:
DUSTIN NGUYEN

GAZE

The man who calls himself Tracy Lone was found abandoned in an alleyway by a Turkish gypsy woman, Amria Gezer. Upon looking into his strange, silvery eyes, she found herself personally experiencing every evil she'd ever committed. Fighting back the surge, she took the babe in and raised him as her own. Now, steeped in the secrets of his adopted people, Lone unleashes the sins of the wicked upon themselves under the alias of Gaze—placing his symbol, the nazar (or "true eye") upon his victims.

CONCEPT BY:
SUNG KANG

PENCILS BY: BILLY TAN;
INKS: WALDEN WONG;
COLORS: SEAN ELLERY

When star cross-country runner Faye Oh loses a close race with a nemesis due to a persistent cold, her grandmother advises her to visit an acupuncturist to "clear" her blocked meridians. The treatment does more than relieve Faye's congestion: It also activates her hidden ability to tap the "breath of the world," the living energy flows that the Chinese call "qi." And now the girl who has always lived for the feeling of wind in her face can ride qi flows through the sky.

CONCEPT BY:
IAN KIM & JEFF YANG

ART BY:
IAN KIM

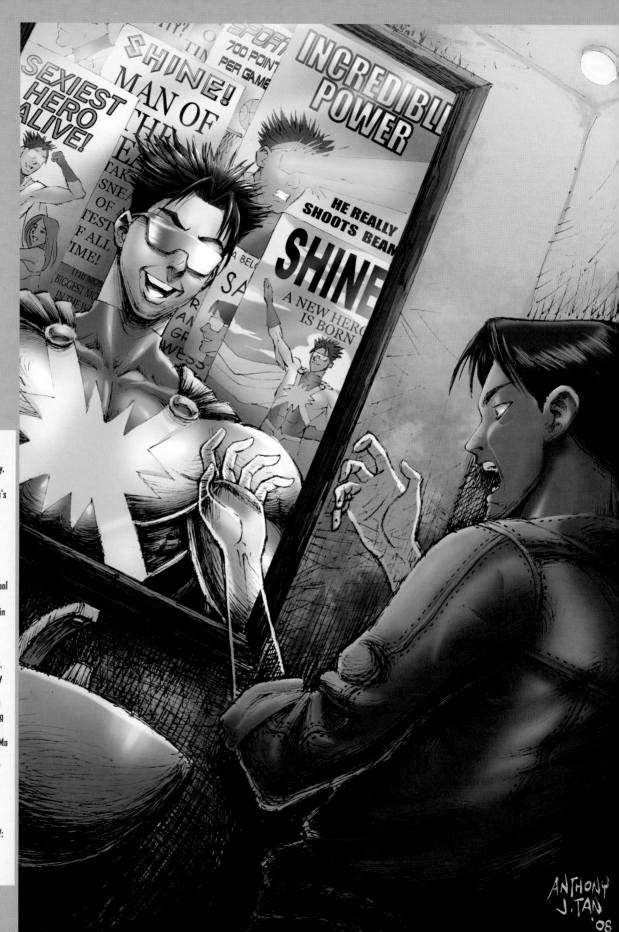

Darren Mo is an ordinary high school student—so ordinary, in fact, that people hardly even notice he's there. Mo's social invisibility is so total that he finds himself literally fading away. After saving a classmate's life and briefly becoming school hero, he realizes his affliction also works in reverse: The raw admiration of his peers grants him amazing new abilities. To keep them, the shy teen creates an alter ego, Shine—an exhibitionist glory-hog who does anything to get attention. But is Mo gaining superpowers while losing his soul?

CONCEPT BY:
LEONARDO NAM

PENCILS AND INKS BY:
ANTHONY TAN:
COLORS BY:
RUBEN DE VELA

When Jia was chosen as the young queen of an ancient Chinese emperor, her adoring husband commanded his alchemists to grant her eternal life. After years of experiments and the emptying of the kingdom's resources, the sages succeeded— once: When the emperor himself tried the elixir, he was instantly killed, throwing the realm into chaos. The now-immortal Jia escaped and went into hiding, where she spent millennia learning every human ability: languages, sciences, and all forms of combat. Now the wisest of the wise and the deadliest of warriors... she is no longer in hiding.

CONCEPT BY:
KELLY HU &
MARK ALLEN

ART BY:
CLIFF CHIANG

CATACLYSM

Since childhood, Dustin Kwon has been an unwilling test subject for North Korean nanotech experiments. Now the billions of nanites that saturate his body give him incredible strength and speed, accelerated healing, heightened senses, memory and intelligence. But these powers come with a price: His cells experience deterioration that the nanites can only repair by decomposing the flesh of other humans. Though he tries to consume only those who deserve to die, his existence is now a constant struggle to maintain not just his identity...but his very humanity.

CONCEPT BY:
YUL KWON

ART BY:
DEODATO PANGANDOYON

John Go is a software coder for a mammoth tech company. Late one night, he encounters a strange old man, who reveals the company he works for is run by a race of aliens. Before Go can call security, the man opens his briefcase to release an odd purple vapor that streams up into Go's mouth, nose, and ears. In a matter of months, the man explains, the invasion will begin, its plans based on algorithms Go himself had unwittingly written. The spirit flowing from the briefcase gives him the power to fight back, offering humanity a slender chance of survival...if he can convince his coworkers that he isn't crazy and subvert his company's plans from within.

CONCEPT & ART BY:
KAZU KIBUISHI

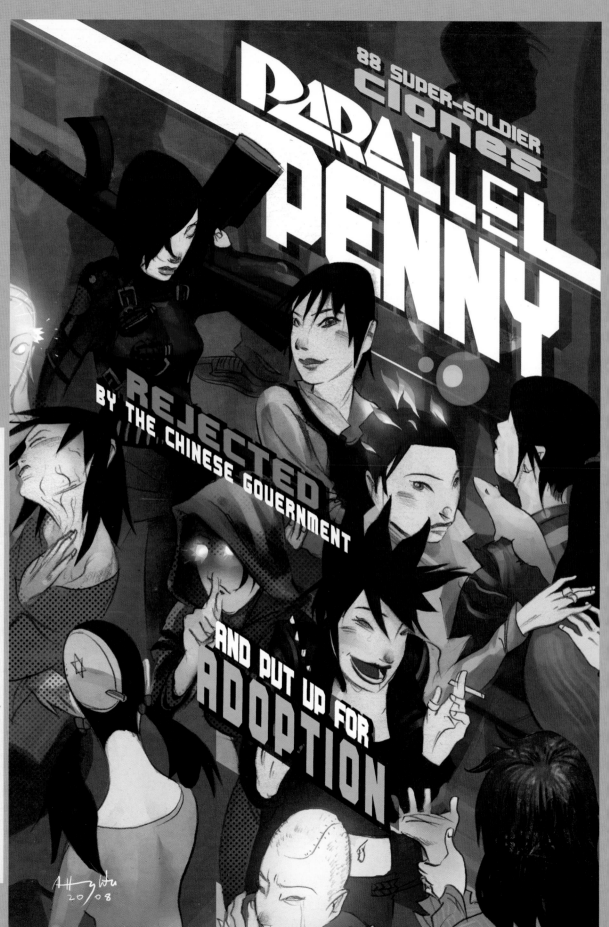

88 SUPER-SOLDIER Clones

PARALLEL PENNY

REJECTED BY THE CHINESE GOVERNMENT

AND PUT UP FOR ADOPTION

Fifteen years ago, a secret Chinese military program cloned 88 identical children from a single cell, seeking to produce the beginnings of a metahuman army. But when the children were revealed to be female, funding for the project was terminated in favor of a new "Socialist Super-Boys" initiative. The military ordered the project's results terminated as well; instead, the scientists in charge mercifully put the 88 "sisters" up for adoption. So the babies were delivered into the arms of loving parents all over the world, and all was well—until the Pennies matured, discovered their powers, and began to explore their past...

CONCEPT & ART BY:
ANTHONY WU

story by: Nick Huang — art by: Alexander Shen

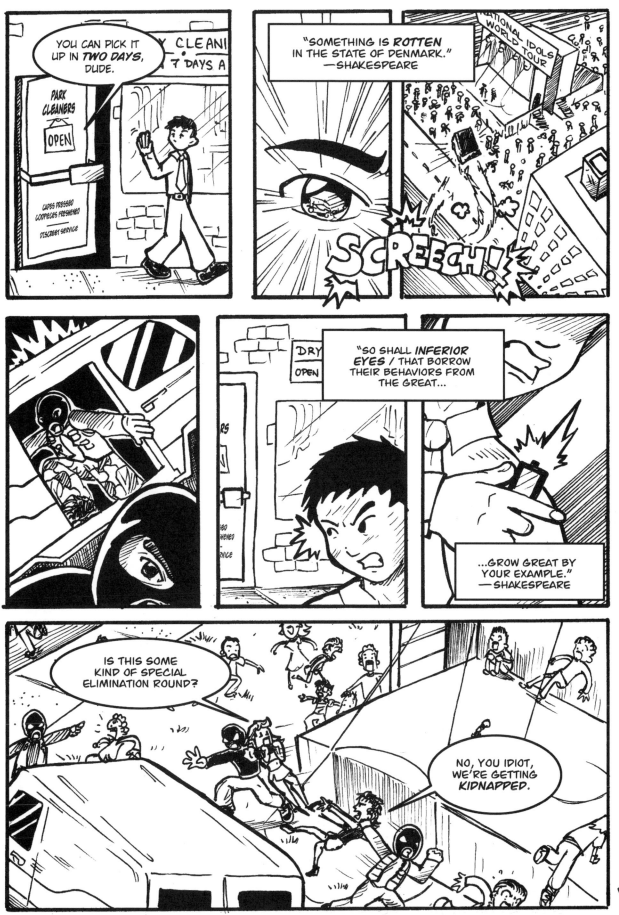

story by: Ted Chung & Anuj Shrestha — art by: Anuj Shrestha

BUT I WAS ONLY PROTECTING HER. FROM THOSE WHO WOULD CONSIDER ME A MONSTER.

I NEVER WANTED TO BE DIFFERENT.

RAJASTHAN, 1958.

147

story by: John Kuramoto - art by: Christine Norrie

story by: Koji Steven Sakai - art by: John Franzese

story and art by: Johann Choi

story and art by: Martin Hsu

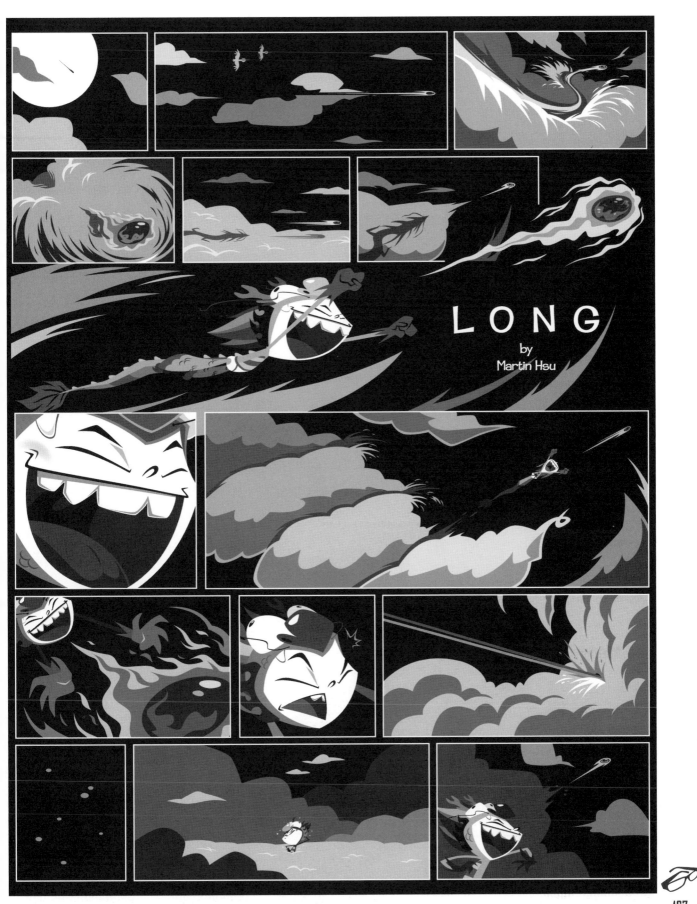

LONG

by
Martin Hsu

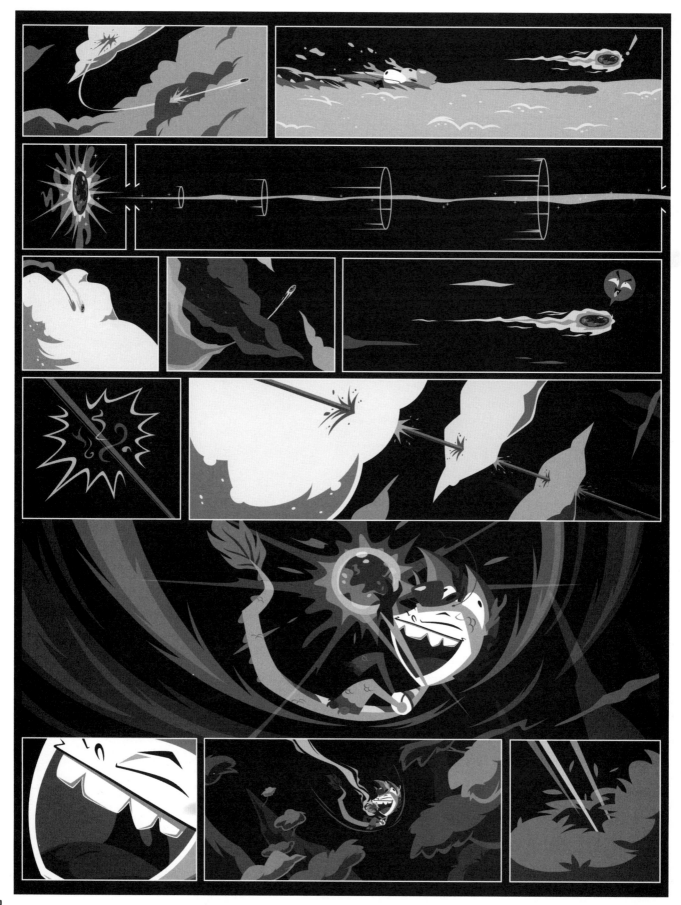

END.

story by: Ken Wong - art by: Tiffanie Hwang

story by: Parry Shen - art by: Sarah Sapang

178

...EVEN APART FROM HIS ULTIMATE SACRIFICE, IT JUST SEEMS SUPERHUMAN TO ME THAT HE DID WHAT HE DID—
—TRAVELING SIXTEEN MILES.
SHERIFF
"HE MADE A DECISION THAT WAS BOTH THE EASIEST AND THE HARDEST ONE IN HIS LIFE— TO SACRIFICE HIMSELF FOR THOSE HE LOVED MOST."
"EVEN THOUGH I WAS ONLY FOUR, I DIDN'T NEED TO HEAR THE REPORTERS TO KNOW WHAT MY DAD HAD DONE."
Richard Kim April 9, 1971 December 4, 2006 Husband Father Hero Whose greatest power came from his heart.
READY TO GO?
IN A MINUTE, MOM...
OKAY, BUT I WANT YOU OUT OF THIS WEATHER...
"...IT CAN'T BE ANY GOOD FOR THAT FEVER OF YOURS..."
SEE YA LATER, GRANDPA...
MATTHEW C KIM
DAL OF HONOR CAPT US ARMY WORLD WAR II OCT 21 1909 NOV 29 1972
Richard Kim
April 9, 1971 December 4, 2006
Husband Father Hero
Whose greatest power came from his heart.
RICHARD JAMES KIM!
COMING, MOM!
END.

story by: Jeff Yang - art by: Francis Tsai

SANTA FE, TWO DAYS AGO

KEIKO AGENA is in Los Angeles training for the day acting becomes an Olympic event. Her coaches at *Gilmore Girls*, *Without a Trace*, and *Private Practice* all say she's got a shot at the gold.

JIMMY AQUINO runs the Internet radio station A Fistful of Soundtracks and writes and draws *The Palace*, a web comic that can be read at afistfulofsoundtracks.blogspot.com. His favorite Chinese food is pizza.

JEREMY ARAMBULO lives and draws comics in Brooklyn, New York. Find him on the Internets at JeremyArambulo.com.

A.L. BAROZA is an animation and comics artist whose recent work has appeared in TOKYOPOP's *Rising Stars of Manga 3* and *Hot Mexican Love Comics 2007*. His online home is www.albaroza.com.

JEF CASTRO is Fil-Am by way of New York. He has several secret identities that he is not at liberty to speak about.

BERNARD CHANG—best known for his work for DC, Marvel, and Disney—signed on to his first-ever regular professional gig based on the contingency that the main character, Dr. Mirage, be an Asian American male superhero who didn't know kung fu. [www.bernardchang.com]

LYNN CHEN is an actress, best known for her role as Vivian Shing in Sony Pictures Classics' *Saving Face*. Lynn can also be seen in *X's and O's*, *I'm Through with White Girls*, and *Lakeview Terrace*, all available on DVD.

CLIFF CHIANG is a huge disappointment to Asian parents everywhere, having squandered a Harvard education and a legal career to draw comics. He is currently working with rock legend Neil Young on the graphic novel *Greendale* and has no regrets.

JOHANN CHOI is currently working on his master of divinity degree at Duke University. Though born in Korea, he's spent most of his life in California, where he somehow developed a taste for country music and comic books.

TANUJ CHOPRA enjoys vindaloo, vintage video games, and any kind of modular furniture that can be rearranged for maximum lounging comfort. His films explore the power of place in shaping a subculture that both challenges and nourishes the individual.

KEITH CHOW's childhood heroes were Batman, Michael Jordan, and Kool Moe Dee. Now, thanks to his daughter, his favorite superheroes are the Wonder Pets.

TED CHUNG is a film director and screenwriter based in Los Angeles. His short films *A Thousand Words* and *On Time* have screened at festivals, including Berlinale and Cannes.

CLARENCE COO is a playwright living in New York City. His work has been seen at the New York International Fringe Festival, Theater Mu, East West Players, Round House Theatre, the Kennedy Center, and the Mark Taper Forum.

MING DOYLE was born in Boston, but her formative years were spent at the nation's oldest co-educational institution, with a brief layover in the People's Republic of China for some noodles. Find more art at mingdoyle.com.

JAMIE FORD is the great-grandson of mining pioneer Min Chung, who adopted the western name "Ford" in 1865, thus confusing countless later generations. His debut novel, *Hotel on the Corner of Bitter and Sweet*, was published in January 2009.

JOHN FRANZESE is in an illustrator living in New York City. John is also a Korean adoptee. As a result, he is often confused on paper for being white and in person for being remarkably good at speaking English. [www.johnfranzese.com]

ERWIN HAYA: With hands, I create.
With fists, I destroy evil.
Who that ninja?
Me.

MARTIN HSU is fascinated by current events, Chinese mythology, and kids with oversized creatures. When he's not imagining flying above the Yellow River, he works in animation as a character designer. Please visit martinhsu.com for more of his silly doodles.

KELLY HU, who co-created Jia with Mark Allen, has starred in *Martial Law* and *The Scorpion King*, and was Lady Deathstrike in *X2*. Her website is www.kellyhu.com.

NICK HUANG originally hails from Staten Island, New York, former home of the world's largest garbage dump. After graduating with a B.A. in biology, he decided the suffering was not nearly enough and is now pursuing an M.D./Ph.D. at Loyola-Stritch.

TIFFANIE HWANG was born in San Francisco, and after a brief stint in biology, gave in to her love of comics and cartoons and studied media arts. She currently works as a production artist for game software and communications.

BENTON JEW began his career as an illustrator/VFX art director at Industrial Light & Magic, working on films such as *The Mask*, *Star Wars*, and *Men in Black*. Now freelancing in Los Angeles, Benton draws comics in his spare time. [bentonjewart.blogspot.com]

HELLEN JO's newest comic, *Jin & Jam*, is currently being serialized by Sparkplug Comic Books. Visit her online at hellllen.org, or write her a letter at PO Box 40846, San Francisco, CA 94140.

KRIPA JOSHI is an illustrator and comic artist from Nepal. While at the School of Visual Arts in New York, she developed her signature character, Miss Moti. [www.kripakreations.com]

Filmmaker **MICHAEL KANG** wrote and directed the movies *The Motel* and *West 32nd*. For more info, visit www.kangisman.com, www.themotel-film.com, and www.w32nd.com. Or you can Google him (he is not the Michael Kang who plays mandolin).

SUNG KANG is just a guy from Gainesville, Georgia, who plays pretend for a living. When he's not busy playing pretend, he's probably slaving away at his restaurant, Saketini, in Brentwood, California. [www.sungkang.com]

KAZU KIBUISHI is the editor and art director of the *Flight* comics anthology series and the creator of the *Amulet* graphic novels for Scholastic Publishing. He also has webcomics posted at his website, www.boltcity.com

IAN KIM has lived in the United States, Korea, Japan, Australia, and Canada. Since graduating from NYU with a BFA in film and television, he returned to the Los Angeles area, where he works at motion design studio Buck. [www.lkplay.com]

JOHN KURAMOTO animated two cartoon shorts for TV's *This American Life* with Chris Ware, an ad for Altoids with Charles Burns, and several minutes of the *American Splendor* movie with Doug Allen. He hasn't written comics in a long time.

YUL KWON became the first Asian American to win *Survivor* during 2006's controversial racially segregated season. He has been active in campaigns to empower the Asian American community through political activism, bone marrow registration, and domestic violence prevention.

GREG LAROCQUE, a working professional artist for more than 30 years, is the founder of Exiled Studio. He is best known for his work on *Legion of Super Heroes* and *The Flash*. [www.greglarocque.com]

CHI-YUN LAU lives in Boston, where he moonlights as a street vigilante and boxing cyborg. During the day, he's a mild-mannered freelance illustrator who enjoys jaunts into the eighth dimension in his rocket car. His website is www.chi-yun.com.

DANIEL JAI LEE was born and raised in Minneapolis. After majoring in history at the University of Chicago, he moved to Los Angeles, where he currently works in television and is an independent filmmaker. He loves Taco Bell.

SONNY LIEW is an Eisner-nominated comic artist and illustrator whose work includes titles for Image, Vertigo, SLG, and Disney, and the Xeric-awarded *Malinky Robot*. He currently resides in Singapore, where he sleeps with the fishes. [www.sonnyliew.com]

JERRY MA became one of the first creators on Digital Webbing Presents, where his graphic short story "Burn" led him to launch the indie studio Epic Proportions with his brothers. [www.epicprops.com]

NAEEM MOHAIEMEN works in video, print, and text to explore historic markers. [www.shobak.org]

LEONARDO NAM's upcoming projects include *He's Just Not That into You*, *The Two Bobs*, and *Watching TV with the Red Chinese*. He has been a lifelong fan of, and is excited to branch out into, the world of comics. [www.leonardonam.com]

DUSTIN NGUYEN is a comic book artist and toy designer living in Long Beach, California. Currently, he illustrates one of DC Comic's flagship titles, *Batman: Detective Comics*, for which he provides interior art as well as covers.

DUSTIN TRI NGUYEN is a Vietnamese American actor. He loves racing his motorcycles, making films, and aspires someday to be able to draw.

CHRISTINE NORRIE, dubbed a "natural storyteller" by *Publishers Weekly*, has earned two Eisner nominations, a Russ Manning Promising Newcomer Nomination, and a 9th Panel and New York City Comic Book Museum Award. [www.christinenorrie.com]

GREG PAK is a writer and filmmaker best known for his award-winning feature film *Robot Stories* and his much-lauded *Hulk* comics for Marvel. He edits AsianAmericanComics.com and writes the "Pak Talks Comics" column for BrokenFrontier.com. For more, visit www.pakbuzz.com.

DEODATO PANGANDOYON graduated from the School of Visual Arts with a bachelor's degree in fine arts. As an experienced illustrator, he is currently working as a background color designer for the Cartoon Network show *The Venture Bros*.

KOJI STEVEN SAKAI co-wrote *Haunted Highway*, which was directed by Junichi Suzuki and distributed by Lionsgate DVD. He is currently working on *The People I Slept With*, a feature film he both wrote and produced.

SARAH SAPANG resides in New Jersey and works as a graphic designer to fund her doodling supplies. Her super abilities include cooking irresistible food and power kicks. See her art at www.bennyville.com.

ALEXANDER SHEN was born in Berkeley, California. After some time saving small children from runaway buses and old people from runaway sandwiches, he decided to retire and pursue a career in illustration and game making.

JONATHAN TSUEI is a writer whose writing is a blend of action, high concept, and strong character arcs. His work can be seen in the anthology *Comic Book Tattoo* as well as the graphic novel *[JUMP]*, both by Image Comics.

PARRY SHEN started on the editorial side of *Beavis & Butthead* at Marvel prior to acting roles in *Better Luck Tomorrow* and *The Gene Generation*. There his grammar got badder having to answer fan mail as the lead characters. [www.parryshen.com]

GLENN URIETA graduated from the School of Visual Arts in New York. He has done illustration work in both Los Angeles and New York and is currently working on several projects (solo and collaborative) in Astoria, Queens. [www.glennurieta.com]

ANUJ SHRESTHA's comics and illustrations explore issues defined by his experience as an immigrant, a Nepali American, and a person of color. He has a diverse range of influences, from the comics of Los Bros. Hernandez to South Indian folk art. [www.anujink.com]

PAUL WEI is an experienced television animator who created the award-winning short *The Old Man, the Zither, and the Dragon*. He is most notably the creator of *Maxwell Wong*, a webcomic about a boy and his grandma. [www.maxwellwong.com]

RAYMOND SOHN exists temporarily in a sliver of time and space choosing to spend his days pursuing art and commerce.

KEN WONG, cleverly disguised as a marketing maven for a major metropolitan licensing agency by day, transforms into a dedicated comics creator, connoisseur, and champion upon returning to his writing/drawing table in Brooklyn each night. For more info, visit www.k-wong.com.

JASON SPERBER, by day, is a mild-mannered online community manager for *The Bakersfield Californian*. But beneath that mask is his true identity: dad to Lucy and Emi, husband to Michelle, and blogger at daddyinastrangeland.com and RiceDaddies.com.

WALDEN WONG is a veteran inker who's worked with DC, Marvel, Dark Horse, Top Cow, Image, *Disney Adventures*, and more. He is located in the San Francisco Bay area. Colors by Sean Ellery.

VINCE SUNICO is based out of Toronto and a member of Spent Pencils Studios. Their upcoming project, *Myth*, will blow your socks off. J.E. Lozano provided inks; Arnold Trinidad, grayscale colors. Visit www.sunicoart.com or www.spentpencils.com.

ANTHONY GO WU has been published in the *Rising Stars of Manga* and *Popgun* comics anthologies. He currently draws a *Battlestar Galactica* manga-short and colors pages for Kazu Kibuishi's *Amulet*. [www.anthonygoes.com]

ANTHONY TAN has been an illustrator for Glass House Studios for two years, where he's worked on *Bratz* and *Couplers* for TOKYOPOP, *C.L.A.S.H.* for Moonstone, and *Roe vs. Abe* for Trepidation Publishing. Colors by Ruben De Vela, also an artist with Glass House.

GENE YANG began drawing comics in the fifth grade. Now, a quarter century later, he is raising a family, teaching high school, trying to pay his mortgage on time, and still drawing comics.

BILLY TAN was born in Malaysia. He's a vegetarian and working on *The New Avengers*.

Author and journalist **JEFF YANG** pens the column "Asian Pop" for the *San Francisco Chronicle* and can be found at instantyang.blogspot.com. Though the discovery of girls led to a brief comics-free interlude in high school, he has never been unfaithful since.

ALEX TARAMPI, since graduating from Pratt, has lived a double life, pushing a wheel to pay the bills and drawing to feed his dreams. He is very happy to be here. [www.theimaginary.net]

TAK TOYOSHIMA is the creator/artist of the nationally syndicated daily comic strip *Secret Asian Man*. Keep up with S.A.M.'s misadventures in race relations at www.secretasianman.com.

FRANCIS TSAI works as a conceptual designer and illustrator in the entertainment industry. He studied physical chemistry and architecture and worked in the latter for several years before pursuing his current career in video game design, comics, TV, and film.

THE ONE THAT GOT AWAY

LARRY HAMA'S "HER"
EARLY ON IN THE BOOK'S CONCEPTION, **LARRY HAMA,** COMICS PIONEER AND THE CREATOR OF MARVEL'S SEMINAL **G.I. JOE** COMICS, OFFERED TO NOT JUST **WRITE** BUT **DRAW** A STORY FOR THIS ANTHOLOGY—A PROSPECT THAT HAD US UNDERSTANDABLY QUIVERING WITH EXCITEMENT.

UNFORTUNATELY, DUE TO LARRY'S RIDICULOUSLY BUSY SCHEDULE, THE STORY HE REFERRED TO AS **"HER"** NEVER GOT BEYOND THE CONCEPT STAGE—EXISTING TODAY ONLY IN THIS **ONE-PAGE INSPIRATIONAL SKETCH** LARRY SENT US ON **SEPTEMBER 19, 2007,** AND IN A FEW PAGES OF NOTES HE SHARED THAT TANTALIZED US WITH A STORY OF **EARTH-SHATTERING SCALE** AND EPIC, **WIDE-SCREEN ACTION.**

"SHE'S NOT A **SUPERHERO,** MAYBE, BUT NOT QUITE A **VILLAINESS**....[SHE'S] A CONCEPT I'VE BEEN KICKING AROUND FOR A LONG TIME." EXPLAINED LARRY.

WE HAD NO IDEA WHAT HE MEANT—AND **NEITHER DID HE,** HE SAID; HIS STORIES EVOLVE AS HE TELLS THEM, SOMETIMES IN **UNEXPECTED WAYS,** MAKING IT IMPOSSIBLE FOR HIM TO GIVE US A PLOT SUMMARY IN ADVANCE. NOT KNOWING HOW THIS STORY WOULD HAVE **ENDED** IS PROBABLY THE **SINGLE BIGGEST REGRET** WE HAVE ABOUT THE BOOK!

OH, WELL. WE CAN ALWAYS HOPE FOR A **VOLUME 2**....

S.I. BEHIND THE SCENES: CONCEPT ART

TOP ROW:
1. BENTON JEW'S PINUP OF JIMSON FROM **DRIVING STEEL** (P. 15)
2. + 3. SONNY LIEW'S CHARACTER SKETCHES FOR **THE BLUE SCORPION AND CHUNG** (P. 63)

SECOND ROW:
1. JOHANN CHOI'S SKETCH OF FURNACE FOR **ON THE THIRD DAY** (P. 161)
2. JEF CASTRO'S SKETCH OF WADE WATADA FOR **GAMAN** (ULTIMATELY DRAWN BY ALEXANDER TARAMPI) (P. 37)
3. ERWIN HAYA'S SKETCHES OF THE HUMAN LIGHT AND TWINKLE FOR **JAMES** (P. 75)
4. GLENN URIETA'S SKETCH OF MISHIRA FOR **THE HIBAKUSHA**—WHO ULTIMATELY BECAME THE "BIG BAD" OF SECRET IDENTITIES (P. 45)
5. JOHN FRANZESE'S SKETCH OF THE BOOK'S MOST POWERFUL HERO, THE IRREPRESSIBLE JUNG OF **MEET JOE** (P. 155)

LEFT:
1. BERNARD CHANG'S EARLY TAKE ON **THE CITIZEN** (P. 56)
2. CLIFF CHIANG'S DESIGN SKETCH FOR THE CHARACTER GALLERY'S **JIA** (P. 133)

BELOW:
3. CONCEPT SKETCHES BY THE AMAZINGLY PROLIFIC A.L. BAROZA FOR **A DAY AT COSTUMECO**: COSTUME DETAIL FOR VAL AS VALENTINE, MECHA DETAIL FOR CANDACE "TIN CANDY" KOH, THE LOVABLE HELL KITTY, AND "NERD BRIGADE" MEMBER KING CON (P. 119)

HARD BOILED FIST — REJECTED

TERRIBLE OTAKU

SHE'S *SO* WELL-ADJUSTED, AND I'M SO... AWKWARD.

AWKWARD GUY

BEFORE AFTER — HELL, NO

Jimmy Nakamura
Ace Plastic Surgeon

OUR FAVORITE "DEAR JOHN" LETTER

WE REACHED OUT TO HUNDREDS OF ARTISTS WHEN WE BEGAN THE PROCESS OF DEVELOPING THIS ANTHOLOGY—AND GOT OUR SHARE OF POLITE TURN-DOWNS FROM VERY TALENTED AND VERY BUSY PEOPLE. OUR FAVORITE "NO" CAME FROM **JEREMY ARAMBULO**, WHO AFTER INITIALLY TELLING US HE'D BE DELIGHTED TO CONTRIBUTE A STORY, REALIZED THAT HE HAD WAY TOO MUCH ON HIS PLATE TO FOLLOW THROUGH.

"UNFORTUNATELY, AND CONTRARY TO MY PREVIOUS E-MAIL, I WON'T BE ABLE TO CONTRIBUTE TO YOUR ANTHOLOGY," HE APOLOGIZED. "I'VE DELAYED WORK ON MY OWN COMIC, 'LET'S DO THIS,' FOR MONTHS, AND DECIDED TO CONCENTRATE ON FINISHING THE NEXT ISSUE BEFORE JANUARY 2008. HOWEVER, I DREW SOME **JOKE IDEAS** WHILE THINKING OF ACTUAL ONES FOR 'SECRET IDENTITIES.'...I APOLOGIZE FOR MY FLAKINESS. GOOD LUCK WITH THE BOOK—I REALLY LOOK FORWARD TO READING IT!"

HEY, IT WAS CLASSY. AND SO, IN CLOSING, WE SHARE WITH YOU THIS PAGE OF JEREMY ARAMBULO'S "**REJECTED HEROES OF SECRET IDENTITIES.**"

BUT THE **BEST PART OF THE STORY?** THIS JOURNEY TOOK SO LONG TO COMPLETE THAT, ALMOST A YEAR AND A HALF LATER, WE KNOCKED ON JEREMY'S DOOR **AGAIN**—AND THIS TIME, HE HAD SPACE IN HIS SCHEDULE TO DO A PIECE FOR US—THE INTRO TO THE BOOK'S FINAL SECTION, "**HEADLINE TO HERO**" (P. 172).

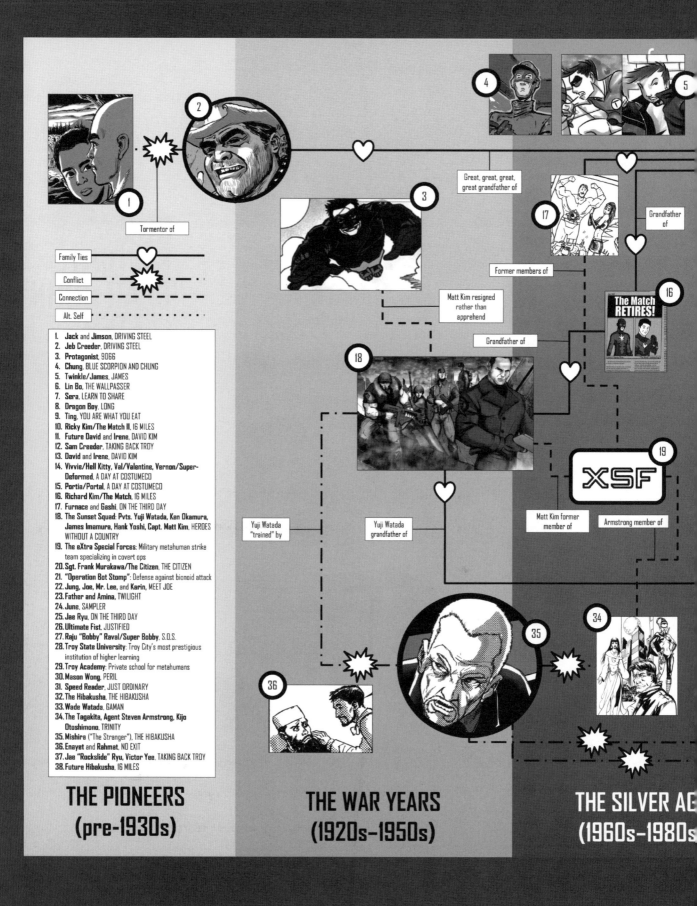

Tormentor of

Family Ties

Conflict

Connection

Alt. Self

1. **Jack** and **Jimson**, DRIVING STEEL
2. **Jeb Creeder**, DRIVING STEEL
3. **Protagonist**, 9066
4. **Chung**, BLUE SCORPION AND CHUNG
5. **Twinkle/James**, JAMES
6. **Lin Bo**, THE WALLPASSER
7. **Sera**, LEARN TO SHARE
8. **Dragon Boy**, LONG
9. **Ting**, YOU ARE WHAT YOU EAT
10. **Ricky Kim/The Match II**, 16 MILES
11. **Future David** and **Irene**, DAVID KIM
12. **Sam Creeder**, TAKING BACK TROY
13. **David** and **Irene**, DAVID KIM
14. **Vivvie/Hell Kitty, Val/Valentine, Vernon/Super-Deformed**, A DAY AT COSTUMECO
15. **Portia/Portal**, A DAY AT COSTUMECO
16. **Richard Kim/The Match**, 16 MILES
17. **Furnace** and **Gashi**, ON THE THIRD DAY
18. **The Sunset Squad: Pvts. Yuji Watada, Ken Okamura, James Imamura, Hank Yoshi, Capt. Matt Kim**, HEROES WITHOUT A COUNTRY
19. **The eXtra Special Forces**: Military metahuman strike team specializing in covert ops
20. **Sgt. Frank Murakawa/The Citizen**, THE CITIZEN
21. **"Operation Bot Stomp"**: Defense against bionoid attack
22. **Jung, Joe, Mr. Lee**, and **Karin**, MEET JOE
23. **Father** and **Amina**, TWILIGHT
24. **June**, SAMPLER
25. **Jae Ryu**, ON THE THIRD DAY
26. **Ultimate Fist**, JUSTIFIED
27. **Raju "Bobby" Raval/Super Bobby**, S.O.S.
28. **Troy State University**: Troy City's most prestigious institution of higher learning
29. **Troy Academy**: Private school for metahumans
30. **Mason Wong**, PERIL
31. **Speed Reader**, JUST ORDINARY
32. **The Hibakusha**, THE HIBAKUSHA
33. **Wade Watada**, GAMAN
34. **The Tagakita, Agent Steven Armstrong, Kijo Otoshimono**, TRINITY
35. **Mishira ("The Stranger")**, THE HIBAKUSHA
36. **Enayet** and **Rahmat**, NO EXIT
37. **Jae "Rockslide" Ryu, Victor Yee**, TAKING BACK TROY
38. **Future Hibakusha**, 16 MILES

Great, great, great, great grandfather of

Grandfather of

Former members of

Matt Kim resigned rather than apprehend

Grandfather of

The Match RETIRES!

XSF

Matt Kim former member of

Armstrong member of

Yuji Watada "trained" by

Yuji Watada grandfather of

THE PIONEERS (pre-1930s)

THE WAR YEARS (1920s-1950s)

THE SILVER AG (1960s-1980s

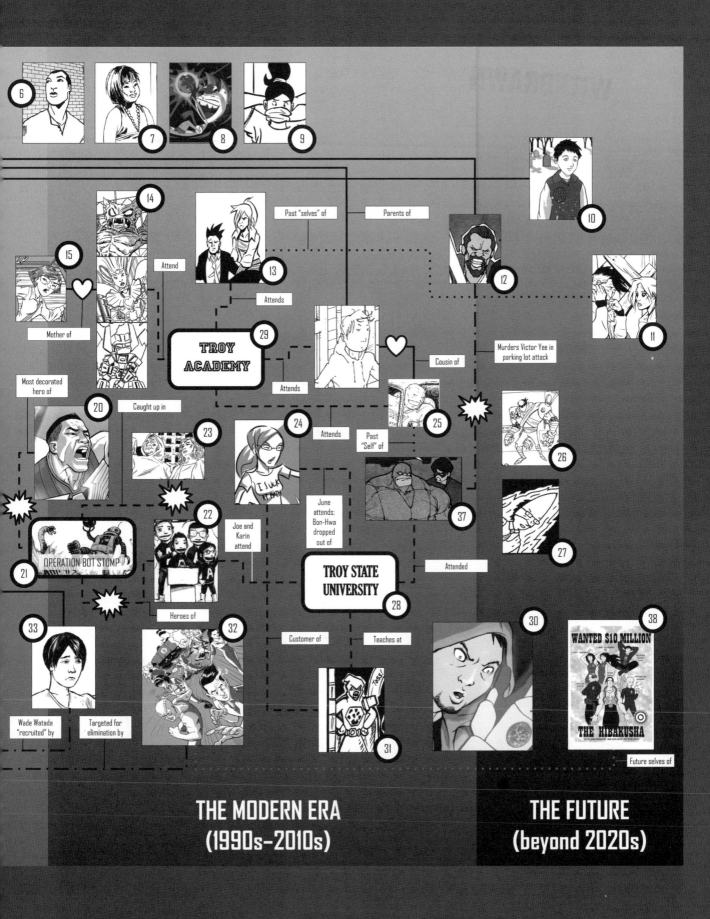

THE MODERN ERA
(1990s–2010s)

THE FUTURE
(beyond 2020s)

WITHDRAWN

Visit **www.secretidentities.org** for updates on new developments with the book and the Secret Identities universe, as well as resources and community related to our creators and characters—including a downloadable **Teacher's Guide** that provides historical and sociological context for the issues and events that inspired many of the stories in this anthology, including:

- The building of the Transcontinental Railroad (**Driving Steel**)
- The Japanese American internment (**9066**)
- The All-Nisei "Go for Broke" 100th Battalion/442nd Regimental Combat Team (**Heroes Without a Country**)
- The atomic bombings of Hiroshima and Nagasaki (**The Hibakusha**)
- The arrival of Islam in America (**No Exit**)
- The murder of Vincent Chin (**Taking Back Troy**)
- The incarceration of Dr. Wen Ho Lee (**Peril**)
- Immigration, representation in the media, stereotypes, and more